Anger Management for Parents

How to Manage your Emotions & Raise a Happy and Confident Kids

Susan Garcia

Table of Contents

Introduction

We have all found ourselves there; you give instructions to your child and repeat them; you implore and assert; you try to talk to him or her like a kid, like an adult, like a friend, and nothing seems to be working. You have reached the end of your patience and the anger is building and threatening to explode. Or maybe your children simply take what you are doing, how hard you are working to provide, for granted.

Raising a kid can often be trying and frustrating. Not only are you solely responsible for the child's future, but you also have to deal with their insolence and lack of appreciation. Balancing all of your responsibilities as a parent while giving your child the care and attention he or she needs to mature into a responsible adult often gives way to anger. And while anger is not necessarily a bad emotion, it can spiral terribly out of control when left unchecked. Anger breeds hatred and sours relationships. It hampers emotional growth and brings serious damage to ever-changing personalities.

Balancing your parental responsibilities and personal life can be very hard when you are new at it. This is why young parents are more likely to experience angry emotions. You will get angry when your kids are running around in a sugar crush and you are late for work or an important appointment. You will get pissed that they leave their clothes scattered around the house and you have to look for them all over. You'll be angry when you have to pitch in with last-minute homework because your baby failed to tell you about it and played instead. You might threaten to leave him or her behind at the store when they don't hurry up; you will be tempted to deliver a smacking to him or her to "teach a lesson", or you might yell and give him or her a tongue-lashing. Any way to express the anger you feel.

The problem with that is that children brought up in angry homesteads or by angry parents develop issues with self-worth and identity. When you deliver that tongue-lashing or threaten a beating, you damage the safety bubble that your child lives in. Because even when the child is making you delirious with anger, they are probably having the time of their life running around or simply having no care in the world. Other methods of punishment like shaking or smacking leads to more serious issues like aggression, antisocial conduct, and mental health issues.

Anger in parents also tends to create anger in children, which means that you might pass on your bad (angry) parenting habits to your child. This creates the unfortunate situation of finding a family with generation after generation of family strife. Even when a child seems to have risen above the angry habits of the parent, they will nonetheless develop deep-seated feelings of anger that they might later pass on to their children.

The purpose of this book is to offer you a comprehensive study of the anger related to parenting. It seeks to uncover all the pitfalls associated with anger management for parents, starting with the different ways that it manifests, its impact, and ways of controlling it. With the knowledge espoused here, you will develop an effective strategy of managing anger in your household – a strategy that protects your kid and you from emotional harm. Knowing how to interpret and deal with different angry behaviors will also empower you to be a better parent.

Getting rid of all the anxiety, frustration, and stress of being unable to deal with your child's anger will empower you to focus on the more important job of ensuring that your child matures holistically. First off, you will learn all about anger. The second thing will be to teach you about your own angry behaviors. The third and final objective is to teach you the different strategies that you can apply to manage anger. This is because having proper knowledge of your anger, especially as a parent, is a very important thing. It is the first step in managing emotions and creating a nurturing environment for your child.

While rearing a child, a lot of the anger that parents feel comes from lacking a proper understanding of children. This is a huge problem that most parents face, with frustration giving way to helplessness and anger that seriously affect the parent-child bond. But when you understand the causes of anger in children and the way children of different ages express their anger, you will be in a better position to offer your guidance and guide your child safely through. And when a child is faring well, the parent will more often than not be doing great. Instead of getting angry at your child for acting out his or her anger and frustration, you can help to solve the underlying issue.

In essence, this book is meant to solve the problem of poor connections between families. This will be accomplished by creating a roadmap for overcoming anger both in yourself and in your child. Only when you have eliminated your anger towards your child will you be in a position to help him or her overcome its own anger. In the following chapters, I will teach you to create a healthy conduit for your anger, find better ways of correcting bad behavior, and understand your child better.

Chapter I :

Understanding Anger

To figure out how to deal with parental anger, it is important that you start by understanding the emotion called anger. It is one of the strongest human feelings and one that is commonly misunderstood and feared. In this chapter, we will discuss all the aspects of anger, including the triggers, its effect on relationships, purpose, and the ways that different people express their anger. We will also touch on aspects of anger that are actually beneficial, laying a good foundation for you to establish a proper relationship with anger. Because for all its ills and harms, anger is inevitable in relationships and getting a proper handle on it, rather than avoiding it, is the only correct way of dealing with anger.

What is Anger

Simply put, anger is a primal emotion that stems out of a need to protect oneself from a deemed wrongdoing. It usually manifests as a feeling of deep antagonism and displeasure. People will either act out their feelings or speak out against a perceived antagonist. Also important to note is that anger falls in the category of emotions that make up a person's survival instincts. The underlying cause of anger is self-preservation. Even when your mind is causing you to see antagonism where there is none, the intention will always be positive. When you think of anger in this way, you will start to see it as something that is meant to keep you safe. You stop fearing it and seek to express it in a healthy manner instead.

But the reality is that anger tends to do a lot more harm than good. This is because like other survival instincts, it has a tendency to take over and cause you to do things that you might regret later. It lowers your inhibitions and makes you say words and do things that you would never do while calm. It is this aspect of anger that requires you to exercise greater control over your expression of it.

Even though they are commonly related, there is a huge difference between anger and aggression. Aggression is the more volatile and dangerous cousin to anger and perhaps the reason why anger gets such a bad reputation. However, there is a huge difference between the two. First off, anger is an emotion while aggression is an action. And it is not just any kind of action, but one that is confrontational. Aggression is just one way through which people express their anger.

Why we feel angry

Anger manifests in different situations, and understanding that it is often a secondary emotion is crucial to dealing with it. For example, when one is afraid, self-preservation causes you to be angry so that you can be ready to fight to defend yourself. The thing about fear is that it is more reactive than it is active. So, it will develop at just the moment when a different emotion is taking root. This is what makes it so hard to figure it out because you rarely get the time to experience anger on its own. You do the things you do when you are angry because of your anger, but the real reason might be fear.

Another underlying emotion for anger is anxiety. Anxiety makes you feel out of control and overwhelmed, which most of us absolutely abhor. To give yourself a modicum of control, the anger takes over and makes you act out. The only problem is that the actions you do when you are angry are often wrong, misinformed, or excessive. Anxiety is especially common among adults. There are so many things that could go wrong, so many ways that you could mess up, that you will find yourself constantly on edge and needing to do something to exert some control over your life. When you cannot control everything, the anger boils over and causes you to act out.

Another emotional aspect related to anger is power – specifically, the need to have and exercise control over every aspect of your life. Power means that you are able to defend against dangers and take charge of your own life. When you cannot get this control over your life, frustrations build and result in anger. This is especially common among adults who faced emotional neglect in their formative years. Power means that you control situations and dictate how they play out.

Even though events in your life bring you to anger, the expression and tendency to get angered depends on your temperament. Everyone has a different relationship with anger. Some people get angry quickly and lose all control. Others get angry just as quick but they manage to stay in control and express their anger in a healthy manner. On the other hand, some people who are slow to anger will blow up once it builds up while others will suppress their anger and ignore it completely then they act out in a different manner. This kind of dysfunctional relationship with anger may cause problems in other areas of life.

The Purpose of Anger

It is very easy and correct to get angry, but people rarely ever get angry the right way. What is the right way to get angry? According to Aristotle, your anger should be directed to the right person, be of commensurate magnitude with the person's err, be at the correct moment, and with the proper intentions. That is where many people go wrong. They are blinded by their angry emotions and direct it to the wrong person, blow innocent events out of proportion, overreact or underreact, or use their anger to manipulate others. Yet anger serves a very important task; that of informing us about our current emotional state. In this section, we will talk more about the purpose of anger in our lives.

Like any other emotion, anger says something about your current psychological state. It is important that you analyze your feelings and determine what message they are trying to convey to you. Even though anger is not the best feeling to experience physically and psychologically, you would be very wrong to ignore it. Yet so many people, driven by the pleasure-seeking tendencies of modern society, tend to ignore most negative emotions, anger included. People with this kind of personality tend to ignore their anger or to bury it deep inside without resolving it.

Other than not expressing anger, another way of dealing erroneously with anger is not letting others feel their own anger the right way. Some people are so uncomfortable with the emotion of anger that they will not let others be angry. This is especially common among spouses, friends, and family members. You have probably encountered that person: he or she would do anything to make up for mistakes (imagined or real) that made someone else even the least bit miffed. It is even worse when one tries to make up for anger for which they are not responsible. This leads to behaviors like lying or cheating just so that a person can get in the good graces of a person they probably should not care for in the first place.

All these reactions to anger are an indication of a dysfunctional relationship with the emotion. It is fear that makes people afraid to express their emotions. Another reason might be that anger is, by nature, an uncomfortable emotion. If you are not comfortable being uncomfortable, then you will have a hard time dealing with it. However, if you can stop to listen to what your heart is telling you in those moments of tingling anger, then you can learn all the great things that anger does for you:

Anger helps you uncover unresolved issues

Sometimes you will get angry when something happens that reminds you of a painful memory. If you get angry when a person says or does something, or something you see in the news, online, or from perfect strangers makes you annoyed, it might point to deeper issues. Whenever you get angry, it is important that you think about the trigger that caused the emotion. If it is something that you can fix, doing so might save you from future anger and dysfunction. If not, then you can work on your way of patching up whatever angers you.

It helps you discover what you need

As a survival instinct emotion, anger can be a very effective way of gauging how you feel about something. I am not talking about the sort of anger that you have to talk yourself into. I am talking about the instinctive reaction you have to an event. For example, how you feel when someone cuts you in line when you are in a hurry to get somewhere, or when you are passed over for a promotion. If your first emotion is relief or nonchalance, then you probably did not want it that much. When you really want something, your reaction to losing it is usually, primarily, anger. The same is true for how you feel when you are doing an assigned task. If your first reaction to a friend or partner's every request is resentful or begrudging, then this might be an indication that the relationship is not serving your needs and you might need him or her to step up.

Anger reveals your boundaries

The fact that you feel irked every time you spot a houseguest wearing your bathrobe or drinking out of your favorite mug does not mean that you are inhospitable. It simply means that you would like to maintain certain aspects of your life unperturbed. Boundary anger mostly manifests as a flash of annoyance that goes away as fast as it came. Sometimes you talk yourself out of it, or you simply distract your mind by doing or saying something else.

However, when you do not listen to your heart and establish clear boundaries, the resentment might build up and explode at the worst possible time. The best idea is always to try to talk it out. Chances are that the person who is crossing boundaries does not think it matters. They would probably not mind being on the other side of that boundary either, so asking will not anger them, as you might fear. It is just your heart speaking to you, and you owe it to yourself to listen.

It pushes us to do better

From the person who works him or herself to the bone to prove to their high school teacher that they have what it takes, to the person who quits their job and starts a successful business, we all want to stick it up to detractors. Anger towards people who tried to put you down, your current bad situation, or the system, can fuel you to great heights. Here, it is all about channeling. You must channel the anger that you are feeling into every activity you do. Use it as a constant reminder of why you must do better and be better.

However, with this kind of anger, you must be very careful. Working for a particular objective just to prove a point is the most time-consuming way to dispense of your anger. You want to make sure that the goal for which you are working is actually worth it and that it is what you want. You must choose your battles carefully and indulge only in activities that benefit you.

It makes your relationships better

You know that cliché that "anger strengthens relationships"? Well, it is not so much a cliché as it is a factual statement. When you fight with someone, you learn a lot about him or her. This is because people, especially people who spend a substantial amount of time together, will rarely ever fight about one thing. A fight about dirty dishes will quickly spiral to neglected needs in other areas. It helps one to understand the needs of a partner, friend, or family member.

As surprising or unbelievable as you might find it, anger actually makes your relationships stronger. Firstly, because it means that a person needs something from you. As long as you learn the needs of the other person and work to take care of them, a tiff will definitely leave you better connected.

Anger Triggers

Anger occurs because of emotionally triggered thoughts creating chemical reactions in the cortex system. These thoughts come from tangible things or events in your life. When you understand the things that set off anger in your life, you will be in a better position to avoid or resolve them for a healthier and more balanced emotional life. In this section, we will discuss some common anger triggers that you can look out for in your life.

Unfairness

When someone does something wrong or insensitive to you, it is very easy to feel irritated or even furious. Unfair treatment can come from anyone, be it your boss, a police officer on the highway, your partner, children, or a total stranger. As a trigger, unfairness stems from that inborn tendency for people to co-exist in an equally rewarding environment. No one likes feeling like they are less worthy, or even seeing anyone treated that way. The only difference is how you react to unfairness. A calm and constructive reaction helps you to deescalate the situation and do what you need to do to prevent a similar situation in the future.

Time pressures

The world is a very busy place. If you look at our roads, you will see evidence of that in the impatient honking and road rage going on. In the bid to ensure that they reach the highest possible level of productivity, people try to save time by multitasking and looking for shortcuts, thus increasing our own stress to get everything done. If you leave work slightly late and have to try to make it to your child's recital in half the time, you are definitely going to be pissed off when someone cuts you off. In fact, studies have shown that tempers are usually a little shorter when we are under pressure. You will be a lot more sensitive to things that normally wouldn't faze you if every second was not so dire. When it comes to time pressures, the key is to plan carefully and follow through on your plans. This helps you to avoid having to rush to do things when the time is running out.

Dishonesty

Dishonesty as a trigger for stress works as a two-way street. First off, we tend to get pissed off when someone is trying to cheat us. This can be anything from a dishonest account of how a friend spent his or her weekend, to someone selling you something of less value than you paid for. Deceit makes you feel betrayed, which arouses emotions of anger and resentment.

The other way that dishonesty triggers anger is when *you* have been dishonest. This is an interesting part of our humanity, being that you get angry with yourself when you are dishonest. The only problem is that people tend to direct their anger at others. When you are keeping something from a friend, you will find yourself snapping at him or her more often. We do this in a misguided attempt to keep the people we have wronged at a distance and to avoid facing our own dishonesty.

Disappointments

Disappointment is a very common anger trigger among people with a mentor-mentee relationship. It is not surprising then that disappointment is the most common trigger for the anger that parents feel towards their children. As a trigger, disappointment comes mixed in with the fear that the other person will suffer the consequences of their poor performance and self-blame for not being able to do better.

In your personal life, disappointment triggers you to anger when you work very hard at something only to have it taken away from you. For example, a business that is doing poorly in spite of all your efforts to keep it profitable, or a failing relationship will both get you disappointed and angry. You might then direct your anger at someone else, be it your business partner, romantic partner, or the world.

Personal threats

We all want to feel good about ourselves. In fact, we spend a lot of time and energy creating a flattering identity for ourselves. And when this identity is threatened, we often respond in kind and come out nails bared. As a trigger for anger, a threat awakens that survivalist, self-preservation part of you. So when someone puts you down or criticizes you in any way, your natural reaction will most probably be to resent them and try to stop the attacks. When anger is triggered by threats to your self-esteem or identity, it usually results in a steaming, latent kind of anger that leaves you in a constant state of defensiveness and irritability. This, in turn, makes you even more likely to get angry at the slightest provocation.

Discrimination and prejudice

Discrimination is a lot like unfairness, but with consequences that are more serious and far-reaching. Sure when someone is unfair to you,

you might get a speeding ticket while not speeding, but with discrimination, you miss a great work opportunity, or face judgment for who others see you as, rather than who you are. Discrimination and prejudice create latent anger by making the victim feel small and incapable.

However, it is not just facing prejudice or discrimination against a person that makes them angry. Sometimes people get angry with someone because they are prejudiced against them. Perpetrators of prejudice and discrimination get especially angry when their victims try to throw their 'inferior' tags off. It is partly the reason why sexist and racist people fight as hard as their victims to keep them 'in their place'.

Expressions of Anger

The way you act after being triggered into anger says a lot about you. Specifically, it indicates how well you relate with your most powerful emotion – anger. People feel and express their anger in different ways. But all forms of expressing anger fall under five major categories namely; aggression, passive aggression, repression, assertiveness, and dropping. All these methods of expressing anger vary in the goal, level of hostility, and the amount of thought that goes into them. In this section, we will discuss each of these categories and the specific actions within them.

Aggression

Some people choose to express their anger by taking it out on others. The fact that aggressive people do not usually take out their anger on the person that made them angry is what makes it such a dysfunctional way to deal with anger. The goal of aggression is usually to inflict maximum harm on another person. It does not necessarily have to be the perpetrator, although most people tend to direct their anger that way. Sometimes, a person just wants to vent. That is why someone may punch a wall, transfer their anger to another person, or just pick a fight with someone else.

Aggressive behaviors usually contain a high level of hostility. This is the reason why people who express their anger through open aggression will have no problem taking it out on another person. Their sole desire is to dispense of their anger on someone or something else, and until that objective is achieved, the anger will remain just as strong and dangerous. Even worse, open aggression clogs the mind and lowers the mental clarity with which a person deals with their anger. This inability to think makes aggressive people even more dangerous.

Moreover, aggressive impulses have a tendency to self-activate; with perceived hostile behaviors acerbating aggression in others. Acting out one's anger does not end your aggression. It only makes it more likely that you will perpetuate the more angry behaviors in the future. These aggressive behaviors include physical violence like punching, verbal assault, and relational harm.

Physical violence

Some people express their anger by seeking to inflict pain on others. The objective of physical violence is usually to exert one's physical dominance over another person to make one feel better. The problem with physical violence is that it only leads to serious legal or interpersonal disputes. Actions associated with physical violence include breaking things, fighting, bullying, and domestic violence. In most cases, these actions are indicative of anger from a different area of the perpetrator's life. For example, children from troubled families tend to get in trouble for fighting more often.

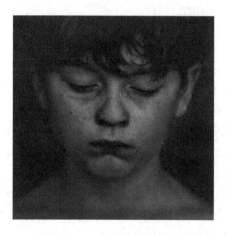

Verbal abuse

When the level of anger is high and a person wants to express it aggressively without physically hurting someone, people tend to use their words. Verbal aggression entails bickering, criticism, accusations, and shouting. Bickering happens when two people exchange bitter words because they are both angry. A war of words ensues in which any form of insult may be hurled at the other person simply so that you can have "the upper hand". Sometimes, when a person is angry, they take it out on another person by constantly criticizing their every move. This leads to a strained relationship and causes the criticized person to lose confidence in their ability to do something.

Another way of expressing anger is through accusations. Here, the quest to find and apportion blame for mistakes turns into a harsh rebuttal of a person's character, behaviors, or personality. Finally, we have yelling as a method of expressing anger through verbal abuse. People who shout generally seek to win an argument more with the pitch of their voice rather than their words, even when they are engaged in other peaceful methods of conflict resolution.

The major problem with verbal abuse is that it causes the same (or even more) level of hurt as physical violence. This is because verbal abuse inflicts harm on a person's emotional wellbeing. For example, verbal abuse from a caregiver, a close friend, or family member can have a serious impact on a person's self-esteem.

Relational harm

Relational harm is common among vengeful people. The idea behind this form of aggression is to teach the offending party a lesson and make them suffer the same way that the offender suffered. A person seeking to cause relational harm to another person will attack his or her relationships, career prospects, or standing in society. Revenge porn falls into this category.

Passive aggression

Passive-aggressive behaviors are those rebellious actions that people do when they are angry but are not expressing or dealing with their anger. Most people who express anger through passive-aggressiveness will never admit to being angry. Instead, they use covert actions and veiled words to show it. This shutting down of communication makes it harder to resolve conflicts and deal with anger, yet the passive-aggressiveness continues to sour the mood and affects relationships. Some of the behaviors include sulking, avoiding people, shutting down, procrastination, and sarcasm. With all these actions, the anger remains to be something that is felt but it is ignored and avoided. It is one of the most dysfunctional ways of dealing with anger.

The reasons why people resort to passive aggressiveness vary. In some cases, the upbringing that the person received plays a part. People raised in families that frown on the open expression of emotions, especially anger and disagreement, tend to develop this form of anger expression. A whole childhood of a person feeling compelled to hide their feelings causes one to find new channels of expressing frustrations.

Sometimes, people with a different way of expressing anger might resort to passive aggressiveness because the situation does not allow the more open forms of expressing anger. For example, it is socially expected that people hide their angry feelings while in a public place or a social gathering. To compensate for this, a person might resort to sarcastic comments, sulking, or avoiding people.

The third reason why people use passive aggression as a way of expressing anger is that it is an easy way out. Passive aggression allows for the expression of anger without any direct confrontations with the people who caused it. For people with a low level of assertiveness or emotionally closeted people, this provides the easiest way of expressing anger without ruffling any feathers.

Repressing

Repression is one of the most harmful ways of dealing with anger. Here, a person keeps their anger bottled up inside, instead of getting to the root cause and dealing with it. A person with repressed anger holds it deep within their subconscious. They completely refuse to acknowledge it and go about life without understanding that the depression, low energy, and cynicism they carry with them is caused by anger. Repressed anger messes with your emotional health and often leads to multiple other issues.

And because you cannot see repressed anger through the common indicators, you should look out for the following signs;

- Passiveness: While most people react to pet peeves and common life annoyances through anger and exasperation, people with repressed anger remain passive a lot of the time. They deny their anger and most other frustrations in life, continuing the habit of repression infinitely. The fact that they do not deal with frustrations in life is what brings about depression and emotional exhaustion.

- Irritability: On the other hand, repressed anger might create greater sensitivity to annoyances. If small things easily irritate you, it might be an indication that there is something bigger you are ignoring. Until you find the real cause of your anger, you will continue being irritable and continue annoying every one of your friends.

- Addictions: Some people seek relief from their anger in drugs or compulsive behaviors instead of dealing with it head-on. Most addicts are simply people trying to bury some deep-seated hurt and anger.

Or at the very least, keep themselves too busy that they forget all about it.

- Anxiety and panic attacks: Today's world is a depressed and anxious place full of people dealing with panic attacks and stress whose cause they cannot trace. A widespread lack of emotional intelligence in dealing with anger means that people do not have an outlet for life's frustrations. Unexpressed anger is a leading cause of panic attacks and anxiety. Deep down, you are afraid that the anger you are ignoring will ultimately catch up with you.

- A negative self-image: Esteem issues are also very common among people with repressed anger. Repressed anger often remains unexpressed because the person does not feel worthwhile enough to express it. They feel that they are not good enough to feel angry or face off with the person that caused the anger. Interestingly, a negative self-image becomes just another thing that the person is angry at – this time with himself or herself.

Processing repressed anger

The only way to get past repressed anger and lead a healthy and productive life is to channel it. You can do this through the following three-step process.

1. Analyze your life and get to the root cause of the anger. Repressed anger often goes back to childhood traumas and misgivings, mistakes you made early in life, or something that someone did that angered you. Think long and hard about your life and think about all the times that you faced disappointments or frustrations. That is a great place to start in figuring out what the cause of your repressed anger might be.

2. Find a way to channel the anger out. Sometimes you simply need to confront a parent, old boyfriend or girlfriend, or a sibling, for something he or she did. Take the anger where it belongs and finally confront it. Even if you just write a text or email and do not send it, just recognizing the anger and the offending party could be enough.

3. The third and final step in dealing with repressed anger is forgiveness. Forgive the person who wronged you and forgive yourself for hurting yourself by holding the anger for so long. This might take time, but you will get to the point of total peace with the frustrating event in due time. Henceforth, you need only focus on the good things in your life, be grateful for the small things, and improve on the way you express your anger.

Assertiveness

Expressing anger in an assertive manner is the best way to deal with it. With this technique, one expresses his or her feelings in a calm and collected manner with the aim being to find a solution. There is also no threat of physical or emotional harm with an assertive expression of anger. Moreover, the assertive expression of anger is more proactive than reactive. Assertive people do not have to be angry to communicate about something that angers them.

Assertive anger is usually direct, honest, and straightforward. It is used to help the other person to make amends and learn how their behavior affects others. It follows the, "I feel...when you" structure, showing in a clear way exactly what part of a person's actions causes anger to another. This fosters a better relationship all-round and a deeper connection as well as forming a closer bond with less anger between two people.

Assertive anger has the distinction of being educative. You can learn a lot about your relationship with a parent, child, partner, or friend based on what causes conflict and anger between you. People who express their anger assertively take the time to think something over before talking about it. This moment of self-reflection and reflecting on an event allows you to gain a better perspective. This is something that lacks in aggressive, passive-aggressive, and repressive anger.

Dropping it

Sometimes the things that make you angry are trivial and unimportant. When this is the case, expressing anger might turn out to be counterproductive. This is where you might choose to drop it instead. Dropping your anger is especially important when you are the only person who suffers from anger. For example, your company makes a decision that negatively affects you and there is no way of getting the decision overturned, or an acquaintance does something to hurt you but he or she does not apologize for it. Or sometimes the thing that makes you angry is too small for you to fixate on, even with the more healthy assertive method of expressing anger.

You must be careful, however, not to mistake repression for the more healthy technique of dropping your anger. The main difference is that with the former, the decision to ignore anger is automatic while dropping entails a conscious choice to let the anger go. You must examine your anger, seek to understand the impulses bring it about, and then release it. However, you must be careful that dropping does not become your go-to move for dealing with anger. While some things are too small to fixate on, do not run from or ignore your anger. Where the situation demands it, express your anger assertively and in a healthy manner.

The Dangers of Anger

When you address your anger in time and in the right manner, it can be a good emotion, keeping you balanced, satisfied, and helping you take care of your needs. But holding anger for a long time, repressing, or getting explosively angry every so often, can all be quite harmful. In this section, we will look at some of the dangers of anger in your life.

Anger affects your cardiac health

Anger doubles the chances of suffering a cardiac arrest for up to two hours after an angry outburst. This is especially so when your anger is expressed in the more unhealthy styles such as repression and aggression. The reason for this is that aggression and repression make you lose control and send your heart racing with adrenaline.

It worsens anxiety

Anger increases the level of paranoia you feel about your life because it gives you an actual thing to worry about. However, it blows the seriousness of an issue out of proportion, triggering anxiety. Anger increases the seriousness of symptoms of generalized anxiety disorder, increases worry, and interferes with your ability to continue functioning normally. Moreover, anger adds hostility to your anxiety, making it even harder for you to let someone in and find a solution to what is troubling you.

It leads to depression

Anger, whether repressed or otherwise, is commonly linked with depression in yourself, or the person affected by your anger. When you experience long episodes of dealing with anger, your life becomes increasingly sadder and miserable. You may feel discontent and low if you're struggling with anger issues. Depression can also affect those close to you if anger is a common feature in your life and it is expressed in dysfunctional ways. For example, physical assault, a common expression of aggressive anger, causes trauma. The victim of this form of anger is more likely to suffer from depressive episodes later on in life.

The Effects of Anger on Relationships

When anger is not managed in the proper manner, it can have some serious impact on relationships.

It creates distrust

Lashing out in anger at someone that looks up to you makes them develop feelings of fear and mistrust. This is especially likely to happen when the subject of your anger is in the subordinate position in the relationship. The fear comes from the feelings of having disappointed someone that a person looks up or depends on. Distrust comes from feeling like the love and loyalty a person gets from another is conditional on them not messing up.

It festers resentment

Resentment is the common denominator in people that suppress their anger or express it through passive aggression. In some instances, even dropping anger can make someone resent another or seek to establish distance. This makes a relationship feel strained, forced, or may make someone feel unappreciated and trapped.

Causes tension and dissatisfaction

Being around a person that might explode in anger at the smallest provocation is one of the most unsettling experiences that a person can go through. A relationship where one person has a tendency to be easily angered by the smallest thing is usually tense and full of frustrations. This is because of the fear that anything a person does or says might cause the other to explode in anger and do something bad. At some point, the unresolved issues mount and dissatisfaction builds until the relationship becomes dysfunctional and strained.

When Anger is a Good Thing

For all its harms, anger can be quite fulfilling when it is handled well. At that point when you are angry and your blood is rushing in your veins, your mind is filled with the injustice of the situation, and you are so bold as to say anything, you are easily at your strongest emotional state you will ever get into. As long as you keep your anger assertive, you can add some force to it to put an end to something that you have been dropping or avoiding for a while. Below are some ways that anger improves your life when it is managed properly.

Increase your eloquence

People are usually at their most eloquent when they are angry. This is because the fear you have of annoying someone is usually less and you can say what you really think about a person or situation.

Improves your ability to negotiate

If you have been living in a repressive environment and have gradually been growing impatient, anger gives you the strength to negotiate for better terms. This could be anything from a teenager forcing his or her parents to ease up on criticism, a boss giving you better terms of work, or a partner quitting some annoying behavior that you have been tolerating.

Anger can be therapeutic

Sometimes all you need to do is yell at someone to feel better about something that has been troubling you. Here, the important thing is that you direct your anger at the right person, keep it proportionate to the issue at hand, and avoid using your words to hurt. The kind of anger that allows you to express your needs, negotiate for better terms, and get your needs to be met actually improves your satisfaction and level of happiness. Just be sure to keep from personal attacks, demeaning comments, or foul language.

In dealing with anger, you must keep in mind that you are looking to manage, not avoid, the emotions.

Chapter II: Anger in Parenting

After looking at anger in the larger context of society, let us narrow down and look at anger at home, and more specifically, parental anger. Parents carry the greatest burden of raising kids and determining how their future turns out. But it is a job with a lot of pitfalls as far as anger is concerned. Taking care of kids can be a very stressful job. On the other hand, anger at home has serious developmental impacts on the child. It is very important that you understand its causes and effects so that you are in a better position to rein it in and bring up your child in a healthy and nurturing environment.

The Angry Parent

Anger has become the emotion that people like to skirt around and never discuss, or when they do, they do so in lower tones. Attending an anger management class is as taboo a topic as rehab and most people would rather not discuss it even with their therapist. Suppressing and avoiding anger becomes the norm, which means that people are usually completely unequipped to deal with moments of anger when they occur. And because children are more vulnerable, they get the worst of this whole anger-avoidance culture. Even if a child will not be yelled at or beat, there is a common vein where parents fail to train their children on anger management. Even worse, parents without the proper anger management abilities give their children the impression that all anger is bad and it is wrong to feel it.

This is the wrong approach to anger management. A better way of doing it is learning how to actually deal with angry emotions. Master your temper so that your child can learn from you how to do the same. Even some good parents who are committed to raising healthy children by employing a conscious and peaceful parenting style struggle with anger management. Sometimes all your child needs to do is mumble something under his or her breath, spill some food, or mess up at school and your hot-headed inner self comes out.

Children will push all your buttons, often at the same time, and drive you crazy. If there is more than one of them, then you can expect your temper to always be just under the surface waiting to explode. And with all those sleepless nights and constant worry that you now have to live with, being a parent can be like navigating a landmine of angry outbursts. However, this problem is not unique to you. Parents have been anxious and irritable for as long as children have been curious and excitable. And I get it, all the worrying about your child's safety and dealing with their mess-ups can you set you on edge. But you can control the way you react to their antics. You can become the more clear-headed and sober one, because that is who you are.

Causes of Anger in Parenting

The relationship between a mother (or father) and her kid is a special one. It is the oldest relationship most people have with another human being, and it is by far the most entitled one that most of us have. Children rarely ever treat their parents with love and consideration. In fact, you might find yourself getting annoyed at the number of times that your child seems to appreciate the things that strangers do for him or her more than he or she appreciates you. Because of this irrational nature of the parent-child bond, it holds a lot of potential for anger.

Even worse, the theory of "the ghost in the nursery" states that children arouse a certain level of childishness in their parents (Markham, 2019). Any parent will either be looking to recreate their childhood through their children or turning as far away from their childhood as possible. This creates a level of irrationality that can cause a lot of friction between mother and child and cause a lot of anger. Understanding the real reasons why you keep getting angry with your child can help you to improve and become a better mother to your children.

When it comes down to it, parental anger does not come because of unruly and mischievous behaviors of children. Underlying factors like fear, repressed anger, and stress play a bigger part in a parent's likeliness to get angry with their kid. That is why one parent with a very naughty child might keep his or her cool while dealing with the child and treat him or her with compassion and understanding while another blows off at the smallest mistake by their child. In this section, we will look at some of the common causes of parental anger.

Expectations

Parenting can be one of the most challenging experiences because, first off, you know that the welfare of your child, both present and future, depends on how good a job you do. Some parents tend to get overwhelmed by these expectations and forget that children are not just tiny adults. They forget that children are going through life with many first-hand experiences. With this comes all those fears that you as an adult face such as the unknown, failure, criticism, and peer alienation. When you think about every situation with your child from his or her perspective, you will be able to unlock appreciation for your achievement in raising a human rather than criticizing their every action.

Here is the one thing you should take away from this whole book: children mess up. This is what they are supposed to do. They would not be children if they did not make mistakes. Even you make mistakes! In most cases, your child is convinced that what he or she is doing is the best thing to be doing. And if not, he or she is just engrossed in the moment, uncaring, and unconcerned, because they trust you absolutely to protect them.

Most parents make the mistake of judging their children using their adult marking schemes. You cannot expect a child to understand that the sun setting means it's time to leave the playground and go home; he or she probably expects you to turn the lights on as you do at home. And when you spend four hours making a gourmet meal at home and your little one asks for candy instead, it might be very difficult to take that insult to your cooking skills lying down. But you cannot possibly expect him or her to have your taste in food. It all boils down to ensuring that you give your child what is best for him or her but that you still understand he or she has a different way of looking at things.

Fear

Sometimes the reason why you are so angry at your child, especially when this anger is never-ending, is because you are afraid. How a child turns out as an adult is a reflection on how he or she was raised, and parents worry about this more than anything else. All parents worry that their children will turn out to be a psychopath or a failure. A small action triggers this fear, which brings about a chain of thoughts that end with your judging yourself a failure in the future. So, you get angry at your future self for what your child is doing in the present, then you direct this anger to your child.

The fear of failure can make you become stricter with your child. And when the inevitable comparisons with other parents come, it is easy to get angry and lash out. On the other hand, your child might resist your attempts at making their future more secure and molding his or her character. This friction creates anger on both sides, further affecting the relationship.

For a parent who had a problematic childhood, the fear of turning into your parent can also make you an angry parent. Interestingly, most parents who fall for this trap grew up under angry parents themselves. With every small punishment you hand out and every disappointing fall of your child's face, you will start seeing yourself as your own worst nightmare – your parents. This only exacerbates the situation and brings about more anger.

Repressed anger

As we discussed in chapter 1 above, repressed anger makes you irritable and short-tempered. Childhood anger and fears make up for a lot of the repressed anger that most of us deal with. Children usually have no clue how to deal with anger and fear. So they do it the only way they can – they ignore it all. This is especially common when the home environment is not conducive for open communication. When a child feels that he or she cannot speak their mind without facing the wrath of the parent, or if parents simply have no time to listen, all their fears and frustrations are covered up.

The biggest surprise you get when you first become a parent is that your childhood anger has been festering under the surface all this time. It is not until your child starts to bite, cuss, or rebel that you begin to think back and discover just how much pain is in your childhood. All that anger comes back to you as a package deal as the "ghosts in the nursery" cause you to second-guess every decision you make pertaining to your child. All these doubts make you frustrated. After this, you will either be too soft on your child to make sure that he or she has is better than you did, or you will be tougher to try to make sure that the child avoids getting in trouble like you did.

And sometimes, you will only recognize that you were reacting to anger from your childhood after you have already yelled at your child and given him or her a time out. As you are asking him to think about his mistakes, you are wondering about your own actions and wondering if it was the right call. Whether you have been struggling with anger in all areas of your life and having a child just made it worse, or whether your anger issues only started after having a child, you will have to resolve your childhood issues before you mess up your little boy or girl's childhood as well.

Stress

Parenting is an expansive job that entails providing, protecting, and mentoring among other responsibilities. In the bid to fulfill all the duties above, you will accumulate a lot of strain and pressure. Even if you were doing okay financially before the kid came along, the medical bills and supplies that you will need to buy will take you down a few notches on the financial security scale. And as the child grows, he or she will continue demanding that you work even harder to provide. To cap it all off, you will have to contend with endless comparisons and, if you are unlucky, complete lack of gratitude and appreciation for all the hard work you do.

At some point, the stress will get to you. Especially if you are a perfectionist, you will get angry with yourself for every small mistake you make. And like I mentioned above, parental anger has no boundaries between parent and child. If you are angry, it does not matter whether your anger is with yourself, your boss, your partner, or the world. Your child will definitely get some of it. Before you know it, you will be yelling at him or her for doing something as innocent as breaking a toy. Marital stress is especially common as a trigger for parental anger. You may think that you are angry with your partner, but your children will get the brunt of it, especially if the partner is not absent.

Angry Parenting Behaviors

Different parents express their anger in different ways. The way you get angry at a child that refuses to eat will probably be very different compared to how you react when your young one hits another or steals. The greater the mistake your child does, the higher your level of anger will be, and thus the stronger your actions are likely to be. Some common expressions of parental anger include;

Screaming

Screaming is one way of expressing aggressive anger. Parents scream at their children when they are frustrated with their behaviors or when you have been saying the same thing repeatedly. Children get as scared of screaming as they get about other forms of punishment as thrashing, especially when there are threats of corporal punishment. Parents who habitually scream at their children only succeed in weakening the parental bond. A child will hardly ever open up to a parent who screams at him or her. It is more likely that he or she will shut you out and become a screamer him/herself.

Hitting

A parent will hit their child in a flash of anger or plan the beating in advance. Either way, the effects of using corporal punishment to discipline your child are all negative. Even though you might succeed in deterring a repetition of similar behavior (not assured though), you will impart serious emotional damage to that child. And even if you hit out instinctively, maybe because your temper rises suddenly, be sure to apologize and make up for it. Hitting your child is an indication of repressed anger or fears and should be an indication that you have personal issues that need working on.

Threats

The things that you say while you scream at your child can show you how serious your anger issues might be. Threats are especially informative because they let you know what you wish were different. For example, if you keep threatening your child with leaving him or her behind, it might be an indication that parenting is overwhelming for you. The same goes for threats like taking away toys or taking away their allowance. You need to review what you say in those fits of anger and determine where you need to take better care of yourself as a parent.

Ignoring your kid

When you have been saying the same thing repeatedly and nothing seems to be changing, or when you are raising an angry kid and he or she does not listen to you, your anger might cause you to start letting him/her do whatever they like. This form of parental anger can be very dangerous because it makes you stop giving parental guidance to your kid. Other parents follow the uninvolved or permissive parenting model (discussed later in the book) and simply let their child do what they please. Most of the time, the permissiveness is simply a failure to pay attention to your kid's needs, which can be just as dangerous.

In fact, parents who neglect their children are very often angry parents. Sometimes the anger might be directed at the world, the parent's parent, or a spouse, but it is anger that brings suffering to a child nonetheless. Healthy parenting means that you care for every one of your child's needs.

Criticizing

A common reason why most parents criticize their children is to make them better. If you make your kid work for your approval but end up not giving them credit when they do something good, it might be an indication that you are harboring some parental anger. You should always be your kid's biggest fan, which means that you let him or her impress you. Because the very fact that she or he is doing something is really quite impressive. However, most parents fail to see this because they compare their children with internet sensations or themselves. What you need to understand is that just like all adults, children are unique. Criticizing makes your child develop self-doubts and low esteem issues.

Comparing

Comparing is one of the most common ways for parents of more than one kid to express anger. Here, you are simply judging one child's abilities against their sibling's and very often labeling him or her a loser afterwards. Comparing comes from a parents fear that one child might not measure up to their siblings. The only problem is that when you compare, you are basically passing the judgment on that baby even before he or she goes out into the world. Your job should be to nurture every kid and allow them to grow into the adult they are meant to become.

Effects of Anger on Child Growth

Most parents ignore parental anger because they just do not understand how it affects their children. But when you think about it, your anger can be a very scary moment for your kid, especially when you lash out. For one, you are probably three times as big as your child is. When you lose your temper and start screaming at your child, you stop being their shelter of comfort and you become an object of helplessness and immense fear; helplessness because there is nothing your child can do to escape from the terror of your anger – you are the provider after all. And immense fear because you are 100% in charge and able to inflict a lot of damage.

Nothing can protect your child from your anger. At that moment, they feel utterly helpless and exposed. Anything that you will do to express your anger will thus be doubly scary. For example, physical violence that is meted out in punishment for a child making mistakes has been proven to have lasting effects in their adulthood. For one thing, children who were beaten have troubled relationships in the future, are more likely to struggle with drugs and substance abuse. They also often have trouble with education.

This is especially common among kids who are terrified of parental anger. When a child is indifferent to his or her parent's wrath, it is usually because they have shut the parent out. Indifference to parental anger is one of the early telltale signs of rebellion. And even though the child may remain "in line" while in the house you provide, he or she will go wild as soon as they are not under you.

However, parental anger does not just affect children while they are young. There is growing scientific evidence of the many negative impacts of parental anger on adults. They include;

Aggressiveness

Adults raised by angry parents tend to be more aggressive and rebellious. The reason for this is because anger was a huge part of their development. When you spend all your formative years under a parent who screamed at you, beat you up, or threatened you, these character attributes will most likely become a part of your personality later in life.

Less empathy

Parental anger is essentially a manifestation of a lack of empathy for your child. Rather than treating him or her thoughtfully and having expectations commensurate to their abilities, angry parents place high expectations on their children and fail to see how these expectations are unfair on the child. This constitutes a normalization of unfairness for the child, so when he or she grows up, she will relate less with the suffering of others.

Poor judgment

Because parental anger judges children's mistakes instead of teaching proper conduct, the children grow up without understanding how to live. They have a less developed sense of judgment for right and wrong. This is why children raised by angry parents break the law almost twice as much as other kids. Tragically, their poor judgment only increases the level of parental wrath the child faces, further exacerbating the cycle.

Delinquency

Because children raised by angry parents are more aggressive, are less empathetic to other people's suffering, and have poorer judgment, they are more likely to engage in unlawful conduct.

This includes actions that hurt other people such as driving under the influence, theft (often with the use of force), among other delinquent behaviors. The corrections system is full of children raised by angry parents who picked the behaviors, took them to society, and paid the ultimate price for it.

Generational parental anger

The worst impact of parental anger is that you will probably pass it on to your child, and they'll pass it on to their children. Remember, parenthood often brings out a parent's own childhood. The memories bring back all the hurt and damage that one suffered as a child, just in time for it to be passed on to a newborn. If nothing is done to end the cycle of parental anger, multiple generations of families might be lost to anger.

Chapter III: The Angry Child

Anger is an emotion just like any other, which means that some people experience more of it than others do. The same is true for children. Sometimes your child will just be mad at you for no apparent reason, which can be very frustrating. A long time of constant disconnection and alienation from your child because of his or her anger will soon get you as angry as them or even more so

Understanding your child's angry behaviors is the beginning of controlling your own anger because anger between child and parent is highly interconnected. In this chapter, we will look at some of the angry behaviors that children engage in and the reasons why they get angry, including the psychology of angry children and anger in different stages of development.

Child Psychology

I have mentioned before that understanding and relating with your child is the most effective way of dealing with parental anger. In this section, we will cover different aspects of the psychology of children. For centuries, society viewed and treated children like tiny adults. It was not until the 20th century that psychologists discovered the differences between a child's way of thinking and that of adults. Even though we cannot all become child psychologists, you can familiarize yourself with the things that make children tick and boost your ability to relate to them. Children experience anxiety, depression, hyperactivity, emotional strife, and attention deficit disorders. But the way they express these issues is more likely to be problematic because it comes intermixed with anger.

Aspects of child psychology

As a parent, you are supposed to harness your child's development in five main categories namely development, milestones, behaviors, emotions, and socialization. Poor growth in any of these five areas will bring issues in life and lead to serious child anger issues.

Development

Children go through development cognitively, social-emotionally, and physically. Of all these developments, the physical aspects are the most predictable. They entail motor coordination skills and bodily changes. However, this area is no more or less important than the cognitive and social-emotional aspects. Inability to exhibit the same kind of motor skills can be very frustrating for a child.

Cognitive development entails the activities children engage in as they collect knowledge about their immediate environment. Children learn language to communicate their needs, start to think for themselves, reason out problems, and start to have a sense of imagination. Cognitive development goes hand in hand with emotional development. As a child learns to listen and talk, and as he or she starts to think for him or herself, they gain the ability to relate with other people and other children. This is where a child starts to develop confidence, pride, a sense of humor, fear, and trust. However, all of these qualities are usually very fragile. Any discouragement might dissuade them from all future pursuits of the same. It is also important to understand that all three developmental aspects are interlinked.

Milestones

Milestones are checkpoints used to measure a child's development in the three areas mentioned above. Milestones allow you to determine the things that your child is supposed to be able to do by a certain age by considering the development arc of other kids. For example, most children start to support their weight on objects by the time they are about one year old. If your child reaches this age without hitting this milestone, then you might need to see a professional child development expert.

Understanding the various milestones from childhood up until your child turns eighteen will allow you to become a better parent. This is because you will have a better understanding of what your child should be able to do at various age brackets. Moreover, instead of comparing him or her with older siblings or neighborhood kids, you will judge their progress on their proven track record of development. For example, you can expect that a child who starts talking a little later will also be later in forming a full sentence, talking to strangers, or interacting freely with other kids. This communication and language milestone is the fourth official achievement that child psychologists track. It allows a child to improve on their social skills and plays a part in him or her finding their place in society.

Behaviors

Children are bound to be naughty and defiant occasionally. It is how they learn the boundaries their parents (and society in general) will not let them cross. So you can expect your child to deviate from your carefully constructed system of acceptable behaviors and habits every once in a while. For example, the terrible twos are the times when most kids start to push the boundaries. This often continues into adolescence and is part of growing up.

It is when your child's behavior changes that you should start getting concerned, mostly because children tend to move towards extremes. Some of these worrisome behaviors include hostility, aggressiveness, or disruptive conduct. They are often indicative of serious issues like oppositional defiant disorders (ODD), attention deficit hyperactivity disorder (ADHD), and conduct disorders (CDs). When the child is going through a stressful situation like getting a new sibling, trouble in school, or parental separation, you should definitely keep an eye out for them.

Emotions

The first emotions that children learn, as infants, include fear, sadness, joy, and anger. As they grow older, they develop other emotions like elation, embarrassment, guilt, surprise, and empathy. At an early age, the turbulence of growth and development makes emotional responses a little unpredictable. This is because children do not have the finely tuned strategies adults have developed over time. According to child psychology experts, some children find it difficult to develop the emotional intelligence needed to regulate emotions. The rate at which a child learns to regulate emotions depends on their personality type as well as temperament and character traits.

It is very important that you understand the emotional temperament of your kid. To do this, look out for signs like the time it takes him or her to calm down after getting agitated. Another thing that can help you understand a child is to observe how they deal with anxiety. Because even though you can understand many of the reasons why your child is acting in a particular way by studying child psychology, there is no one-size-fits-all system of interpreting a child's behavior. Every child is as unique as his or her DNA. Be sure to keep that in mind at all times.

Socialization

Children start developing a personal identity very early in life. Testing this identity against society is what gets a little tricky. It requires that a child develop the skills and knowledge of relating to others. Another important area of socialization for kids is gaining an understanding of where one stands in the immediate family, local community, and at school. The process of discovering where they stand in relation to parents, siblings, and schoolmates can be very challenging for children. This is especially because they have to deal with disapproval, competition, and emotions like jealousy and loss.

The bond between child and parent or primary caregiver is the very first relationship that they form. It informs the kind of relationships a child will form with the outside world. Interestingly, socialization skills like conflict management have the greatest potential to bring a child out of anger. For example, teaching a kid compromise, bargaining, and turn-taking can help him or her to maintain a harmonious relationship with peers.

Context of child psychology

As I mentioned above, child psychology is not a uniform concept. It all boils down to the individual child. However, the context in which you are raising your child often informs their development curve. Behaviors, emotions, and skills that are necessary in some social groups may be completely unimportant in others. In the same way, some cultural groups prioritize some skills over others. Finally, you must understand the limitations brought about by your socioeconomic class as you seek to understand your child's psychological state.

This means that you consider the environmental conditions in which your child is growing. Here, you must be very careful to raise your child according to your surroundings now and not the background or the conditions in which you were raised. Most parents make this mistake and only succeed in confusing their children. Your child must relate to his or her environment and not the stories you tell of "when I was young".

Social context

Children learn to think, gain knowledge, and grow based on the relationships they develop with their peers and the adults around them. A nurturing environment will allow your child to grow up healthier emotionally, intellectually, and physically.

Culture

The social values, customs, and beliefs that a child grows up with inform his or her development. The most important aspect of culture in child development is the relationship with the parent, educational systems, and trends in childcare. For example, the concept of corporal punishment might be acceptable in some cultures but highly frowned upon in others.

Socioeconomic situation

A child raised in a rich household learns different things about life compared to one who is raised in a poorer home. For example, the ease of acquiring toys and other playthings has a huge impact on a child's emotional growth on things like entitlement, self-image, and gratification.

Causes of Anger

As a parent, you are supposed to keep up with your child's development and help them to grow in a holistic manner. Because children usually have not developed the full range of communication and self-expression tools that adults use to get their needs met, they tend to resort to anger as a means of expressing their needs a lot of the time. When your baby was a toddler, your mother instincts would help you to interpret different angry cries accurately. However, as your child starts developing a whole life of its own with friends, school, and hobbies, you might find yourself falling short.

But, keeping in mind that anger is never a stand-alone emotion, you can find out the real source of your child's frustration by digging just a little deeper. And if you can get to the antecedent or the real cause of the anger, you will nip your child's anger in the bud and allow him or her to live a lot more happily. Sometimes there might even be more than one antecedent to your child's anger and you must look behind the first one to reach the real cause. In this section, we will turn our attention to some of the common causes of anger in children.

Hurt

This is the most common and universal cause of anger in children. Hardly any child will remain calm after getting hurt. Unless a child has been taught to suppress his or her pain by the parent, they are usually pretty honest in their expression of hurt. Common things that might hurt a child include being neglected, the feelings of rejection, losing a friend, or feeling like his or her parents prefer a sibling over them.

Sadness

Children care a lot about the people and things around them because they make up their entire universe. The people in this universe include his or her playmate, parents, and close family. Things like school, the family house, and toys make up part of the universe. A child will be the saddest when this universe is threatened. A playmate moving away means that he or she will have either to play alone or find a new friend, which can be a terrifying experience. Other changes like separation and divorce, moving houses or school, or death are also very distressing.

Moreover, children usually have little to no say in the making of decisions that matter most to them. For every one of the changes that affect them, there is the added aspect of helplessness that follows because their opinion is rarely ever considered. Sometimes when your child is lashing out or throwing a tantrum, it is some of the emotions that might be finding their way out. Look out for the things that triggered an angry outburst for a clue behind the real cause of anger. You can then pinpoint the source of anger and find a solution to that. For example, you can introduce a child who lost a playmate to new friends, or you can paint your child's bedroom the same as the old one to lessen the feelings of loss.

Fear

Just like adults, children worry about their wellbeing and that of others. For example, some children get angry when they see their parents or loved ones struggling with an illness. In fact, a child is more likely to get angry when there is an ill family member than when they are sick themselves. Children of parents in dangerous careers like firefighters, the police, and soldiers also fear for the safety of the parent, especially when they realize just how dangerous the job might be. For example, a child witnessing their father in a risky situation, even if their job is reflected on television, will get very upset and angry. The child might then withdraw and avoid the parent to try to protect him or herself from any possible future hurt.

Frustrations

Children have to learn everything that adults take for granted, including movement, communication, and fine motor skills. They also have to witness as their bodies grow as they get older. At the same time, they will be comparing themselves to their peers in the house, at school, and in the playground. When a child lags behind in reaching some development milestone, it is very common for him or her to get frustrated. The frustration manifests as anger and tends to last quite a long time.

Children with physical, emotional, or intellectual limitations are especially susceptible to anger and frustration. They feel like everyone is judging them and that their parents are disappointed in them. But even more serious, they judge themselves and feel inferior to their peers. This anger will probably continue until a child overcomes frustrations and accepts him or herself.

Guilt

Children do not usually have the finely tuned range of emotions that adults have. So when a child is feeling guilty for some mistake that he or she made, the first instinct is usually to lash out.

Sometimes children will even feel guilty about problems they did not cause, such as a death or their parents divorcing. When you instruct your child to do something and she or he is unable to do it or forgets about it, this guilt will probably manifest as anger. This is especially tricky because you will probably be angry at yourself. The way you handle such a situation affects the parental bond you form with your child as well as their emotional development.

ADHD

Children that have Attention Deficit Hyperactivity Disorder (ADHD) tend to have serious challenges doing simple activities that other kids their age do with ease. The constant embarrassment and frustrations of performing worse than other children on ordinary tasks make them more likely to lash out and withdraw. The situation is exacerbated even further by parental frustrations and lack of compassion for their situation.

Embarrassment

A child who is feeling silly or awkward in a social situation and a child who just performed badly in a baseball game are likely to react the same way – by getting angry. Some children get angry when they are embarrassed and might even cry or hit whatever is closest to them. The fear of being judged makes them lash out in anger to distract themselves from their disappointment with their own behavior.

Angry Behaviors

Children display their anger in different ways. Some of the ways that children express anger can be interpreted as normal child behaviors, which is why some parents overlook them and fail to look for the underlying cause of anger. It is important to recognize anger in your kid while he or she is still young and she or he has not learned to mask the anger or hide it completely from you.

The sooner you find the underlying cause of angry behaviors, the easier it will be to solve the underlying problem. It is also important that you deal with your child's anger issues appropriately.

Overreacting to an episode of anger might give your child the wrong idea about expressing anger. It is when your child forms a pattern of angry behaviors that you should be concerned. Isolated incidences, however serious, are usually a pure expression of anger by a child who does not really know how to express his or her anger. Take these moments as teachable moments and teach your child to express their anger correctly.

Children develop anger management issues when they suppress emotions like grief, fear, and hurt. The vulnerability that these feelings bring terrifies a kid and makes him or her defensive. This defensiveness makes children defiant, even cruel. Everything a child does to suppress vulnerability will always be intended to assert his or her independence. While she or he is locking you away to show you that she or he does not need you, it is all just a disguised cry for help.

Withdrawal

Sometimes a child just wants to talk to his or her dolls or be alone, and this is perfectly normal. As long as a child is enjoying their own company, lonesomeness is not a problem. It becomes a problem when your child stays alone but does not seem to be enjoying it and is sad a lot of the time. Kids who feel like their problems are not recognized or appreciated by their caregivers tend to express their anger by withdrawing. A child will express reluctance to family activities, spend a lot of time alone, and lock himself in rooms like the bathroom or their bedroom alone. A child who does not have many friends and plays alone might be dealing with some serious anger issues and in need of intervention.

Temper tantrums

A two-year old child having a temper tantrum where he or she kicks and hits at everything in sight because you did not buy her the toy he or she wanted at the mall is quite common. In fact, this is a very common habit of children in the terrible twos. It is when your nine-year old does something like that, you should really be worried. Generally, you must see an improvement in your child's ability to handle disappointments when things do not go his or her way. It is just a part of the growth in their emotional and behavioral capabilities.

Irritability/impatience

An impatient child wants to get what he wants "right now!" and not a second later. He or she will make a fuss and become irritable any time there is a delay. This goes for anything from a juice box coming out of the fridge to getting a toy delivered after buying it online. Irritability usually indicates frustrations in other areas of life, such as reaching development milestones. The irritability will probably continue until he or she gets to the same level as his or her peers unless you intercede and help him or her resolve the issues causing the frustration.

Aggression

Children have a whole arsenal that they use to get their needs met. These include pouting, crying, and self-pity among others. All these actions are meant to make you take pity on their cute faces and give them what they want. And most of the time, it works like a charm. Children rarely use aggression to get a parent's attention, and only as an absolute last resort. However, some children go straight to the kicking and lashing out. When aggression is the first tool that your child uses to try to get his or her way, then it might be an indication of unresolved fears leading to anger.

Aggression in children is usually an indication of anger at the most distressing levels. With violent behavior, the child is usually feeling pretty helpless and vulnerable. And along with violent behavior like kicking and biting, you will start to see him or her engaging in destructive behaviors. This includes things like smashing toys, tearing books, and chucking away food (often at other people's heads) among other things. Destruction of property is usually the loudest cry for help and indicates that your child needs special help, especially when the behavior is consistent and intentional.

Fighting and bullying

The occasional tussle over a swing at the playground can merely be an indication of a strong-willed or dominant kid. As long as you teach him or her to be more aware of other kids' needs, there should be no trouble there. What you should look out for is a growing habit of getting into confrontations with other children. Especially worrisome is a child picking fights with older children. It is usually an indication that a child wants to prove him or herself, often due to frustrations in attaining developmental milestones.

The most serious indication of child anger, however, is harassment and bullying. A child that uses his or her physical superiority to torment other children will usually be dealing with serious personal issues. One major cause of bullying is frustration from a lack of parental attention.

Insults and bad language

When you do not teach your child to handle his or her anger in a productive manner, it is very likely that it will burst through the surface with explosive insults. When anger remains unresolved for a long time, the occasional insult gives way to foul language that usually comes in explosive outbursts. Children raised by angry parents often notice and adopt the habits of their parents, such as insulting others and cussing. However, the insults and cussing are usually a veneer to cover up their fears and very often self-blame for the strife around the house. In the early teenage years, children will have started to model the behaviors of their parents, including physical violence and drug use due to the frustrations of a difficult home situation.

Hurting animals and other children

Children are usually very gentle with animals like pets. Any form of cruelty like hurting an animal indicates that a child has some unexpressed anger that he or she is repressing. It is both a cry for attention and a grossly misguided way of trying to alleviate the anger inside. In many cases, seeking to hurt an innocent animal, as well as nastiness towards a younger sibling indicates that a child may have been or felt abused. It is a way of paying back a physical assault in kind.

Reflexive opposition

When a child is angry with his or her parents, they are more likely to refuse to follow instructions out of spite. Children get hostile when they are angry at some unfairness that they cannot do anything about. The only way to even out the score becomes rebellion. The same goes for vengefulness. A child who is constantly seeking revenge against people who wrong him or her (peers or adults) is usually fighting back against the anger he or she feels for being misunderstood or a parent treating him or her with no compassion. This is very common for children who have grown up under a strict parent and received disciplinary action for every mistake they made.

Blaming others for mess-ups

A child who is constantly blaming others for mistakes is usually hiding their anger at having disappointed him or herself. It might also be caused by the fear of consequences for mistakes.

Probably, you have been harsh in your punishments for mistakes before and your kid is just terrified of facing the consequences of his or her actions.

Constantly losing friends

Another behavior that indicates sign of anger in a child is the inability to hold on to friends or playmates. Losing friends usually indicates that a child has lower socialization skills compared to his or her peers. The anger develops because he or she will always be losing old friends and trying to make new friends.

Anger in Different Stages of Development

Children feel and express their anger differently at different stages of development. A proper understanding of the changes that take place as your kid grows, as far as expressing anger is concerned, is very important. It allows you to remain as your child's protector by taking care of their needs and to soothe their hurts.

Toddlers have very basic needs of food, sleep, good health, and play. Their range of emotional expression goes as far as expressing needs and calling for help. Crying is the primary means through which babies express their needs. But do not think that only the four basic needs listed above distress your baby. Sometimes, loud noises and restrained movement can make your baby perpetually uncomfortable and weepy.

From the age of three and four, babies are starting to engage in a lot more social interactions. They might be attending preschool, playing with other kids, and spending time with secondary caregivers like babysitters. Children at this age can be very protective of their stuff, including personal space and possessions like toys. They also tend to be possessive of their close relations. A child might not understand that you need to split your attention between him and work or other siblings. This clinginess can be the cause of many tantrums.

At about six and seven years of age, a child will be a lot more independent from the parent or the primary caregiver. Their frustrations will start coming from school expectations and their personal development. At this age, physical expressions of anger take precedence over verbal ones. And because a kid this age has a good idea of what is expected of him or her, and can see when they hurt other people's feelings, they will tend to get angry when they do something wrong and feel bad about it.

In the preteen years, children are usually forming an idea of the self. The socioeconomic status of the family will become either a source of grief and anger or a point of pride. At the same time, a child's social standing becomes so much more important when they start to develop romantic notions. This means that issues of body image take a lot more prominence in your child's life. A lot of the anger that preteens feel is self-imposed and comes from judging themselves too harshly.

The teenage years are the most turbulent of all. Most kids will be branching out on their own and forming opinions, views, and visions of their own. Some teenagers go through puberty without dealing with anger issues. But when there are issues, you can expect your teenager's friends to become even more important to him or her. It is quite likely that you will feel shut out. Depending on the kind of adolescence that your child is having, your teenage child will either shut you out completely or barely tolerate your presence in his or her life.

Chapter IV: Parental Anger Management Skills

It is one thing to understand why your child is acting the way they're acting, but it is another thing altogether for you to hold your own anger in check. Managing your skills becomes especially problematic when your child is acting out consistently and nothing you do seems to be helping. The thing about parental anger is that it comes in flashes when your fears and stresses catch up with you. Sometimes you try so hard to stop yourself from getting mad or lashing out, only to end up hurting your relationship with your child by doing just that.

In the second and third chapter, we talked about parental anger and child psychology. You learned to interpret your child's anger based on the emotions that bring it about, which is the cheating code to parenting angry kids. In this chapter, we will discuss the exact skills and strategies that will allow you to manage your parental anger. This is because anger management skills allow you to hold yourself back from exploding with anger when your child is acting out or being naughty.

As you develop your skills, you will learn very quickly that the ability to keep a clear head when your child is creating trouble is one of the most important skills for effective parenting. It means that you keep being a mother or a father and that you think about what is best for your child even when he or she is driving you mad with anger.

Importance of Managing Parental Anger

Managing parental anger is critical to nurturing a good parent-child bond. A single bout of anger that is expressed too aggressively can undo years of trust cemented between you and your child. An incident of anger makes it more likely that you will experience (and express) more anger in the future. The best way to deal with parental anger is to nip it in the bud. Only then will you be in a position to establish a relationship with your child based on trust rather than fear. There are other reasons why maintaining a level head when dealing with your child is of the utmost importance:

It improves the growth and development of your child

Parental anger hampers the growth of a child by exposing them to aggression early in life. Moreover, most parents get angry with children because they fail to understand the reasons behind common child behaviors. Failing to understand how children act in various stages of their growth and development, or misunderstanding the source of child anger, is a common trigger for parental anger. You will probably react with a punishment when you are supposed to be offering parental support. The wrong reaction to a child's cry for help will make him or her more likely to keep things to himself and suppress his anger. And as we discovered in chapter two, suppressed anger is not a very attractive prospect.

But when you are able to manage your parental anger and are actually there for your child when he or she needs you, you will succeed in creating a nurturing environment for them to grow up. Your child feels loved and protected when you can look beyond his or her anger to see the real reason why they are being fussy. As a result, he or she will go through the stages of growth and development in a healthier and more robust way.

Provide support in times of crisis

Parental anger becomes an all-round easier emotion to handle when you recognize the fact that children mess up. It is in their nature to mess up because they do not know any better. Even when your child is rolling on the floor throwing a tantrum because you did not buy him or her ice cream when it's 15 degrees outside, your expectation that he or she would handle that disappointing piece of news any better is more unreasonable. In his mind, there is no reason why he should not have ice cream any time he wants, especially when mommy or daddy is around to provide. Only you know that the cold might affect his health.

You should teach your child to be a better person, but keep expectations down and understand that he or she is experiencing many of the things for the first time that you take for granted. This way, you will still be supportive when he or she messes up. Your ability to handle your child's messes will determine whether he or she comes to you when things go awry. The ability of a parent to keep a cool head after her child messes up depends on the ability to manage your anger. Children feel remorseful for messing up more acutely than you give them credit for. It does help to have the support rather than the wrath of their caregivers.

In fact, poorly managed parental anger tends to dissuade children from going to their parents when in deep trouble. Instead, they try to solve the problem themselves – and often succeed only in making it worse than before.

Break the cycle

If you are lashing out at your child in anger because you hold repressed anger from your childhood, gaining a grip on those feelings is even more important. This is because you are continuing a system of generational anger being passed on from parent to child. You need to evaluate the source of your anger and make sure that your own childhood is not coming into play. And whatever the case, endeavor to calm down and be supportive of your child instead of being angry at their mistakes all the time. Every time your child receives compassion instead of anger for mistakes he or she made, you will be wiping the slate clean and improving life for generations of your family to come.

Some parents go through parenting without questioning the way they are doing it. They merely do what feels right with every situation. However, most parents make the conscious decision to bring up their children the same way they were raised, or choose to raise them completely differently. This is a very important question because it addresses your own childhood experiences, which always come into play when you are a parent. You should think about your childhood in a critical and objective manner before deciding to raise your child the same way or differently. This way, your parenting habits become deliberate rather than accidental. If there is any anger there, you will be in a better position to avoid passing it on to your child.

Give your child a chance

As we mentioned before, parental anger has the tendency to make children more aggressive, less empathetic, and more delinquent. Children raised by angry parents also have more trouble maintaining stable relationships. You are passing this legacy on to your child by letting yourself be manipulated into anger by his or her actions. Every time you get angry with your child and you lash out, you increase the probability of him or her rebelling against you and against the system. In the same way, managing your anger and offering support rather than lashing out allows you to nurture and mentor them into a more healthy adulthood.

Improving Your Wellbeing to Improve Your Parenting

Parental stress has a huge impact on the wellbeing of your child. Moreover, being as emotionally connected as she or he is to you, your child will pick up on all the things that stress you out. Parental stress is one of the leading causes of stress and anger in children. While you are arguing with your spouse in private and hoping that your kid does not pick up on the tension around the house, your child is worrying about your wellbeing behind your back. If there are siblings, they are probably speculating on the cause of your stress and worrying that the family might be separated.

And while it is your natural instinct to protect your child from the stress of your 'grownup problems', it is their natural instinct to be curious and to want to know everything that is going on around them. And even though your kid never mentions anything that she or he observes around the house, you can be sure that they notice everything. Only when the pressure from all the unspoken problems gets to him or her will a child start to lash out.

Moreover, stress affects your mental and physical wellbeing and increases the chances that you will lash out at your child. While you are busy keeping your 'grownup problems' from your child, the toll it takes on your mind and your body increases the chances of screaming at your child by about 50%. Stress in other areas of your life always tickles down to the people you love, be it your spouse or your child. In this section, we will discuss some tips you can follow to improve your wellbeing and reduce the chances of you getting angry with your kids.

Reduce exposure to negative media

It is normal for parents to worry about the kind of world their child is growing up to find. This leads to fixation on news and current events, which are often negative and alarmist. And while your intentions in keeping up with current events might be pure, the effects are often negative. People tend to notice bad things about others a lot more when they have been exposed to negative media. This includes negative economic news, political catfighting, news of tragedies, and economic insecurity. A piece of negative news activates the fight or flight instincts and makes you more responsive to threats, perceived or real.

And while this may be a good thing in some instances, the last thing you want is to become a hawkish parent that only notices the bad things that a child does. Moreover, negative media increases your level of anxiety, making it more likely for you to resent your parental responsibilities. Any signals that set off the alarm bells in your mind have no place in your life and ought to be turned off as soon as possible.

Focus on the good in every situation

Negative news sends you into a tailspin and invokes the flight or fight response, but positive news calms you down and improves your sense of security. Just one piece of good news on Monday can put you in a good mood for the rest of the week. When you are in a good mood, you will be in a better position to notice your child's needs and respond to them appropriately. Moreover, you will be less likely to lash out in anger when he or she messes up.

The good news is that even looking for the good in a bad situation brings the same benefits as genuinely good news. If you can manage to turn bad news around and find the silver lining in every dark cloud, you will reap the benefits of an exuberant mood. At the very least, you will avoid falling into a tailspin of a bad mood and irritability every time something bad happens.

Budget your time well

A lot of the stress that comes with parenting entails budgeting for twice the number of activities into the same amount of time. For example, mornings are the most stressful because everyone in the family needs to shower, dress, and eat breakfast before leaving the house. You then have to figure out a way to get everyone where they need to go – children to school and parents to work – in time. The strain of a hectic morning can leave you feeling drained and unhappy for the rest of the day, which means that family time in the evening will probably be just as tense as the morning.

All this stress can be avoided if you budget your time better. Start preparing for every day in advance and in the evenings, get everything where you will need it for the next morning. Even if you spend a lot more time preparing for the morning after work, the satisfaction of knowing that you have every aspect of the morning covered will leave you feeling relaxed and ready for the next day. You can take some fulfilling time off, sleep better, and handle the next morning's rush hour more in control.

Reconsider

Stressful things will happen regardless of the number of positive thoughts you have or your ability to look at the good in every situation. However, this does not mean that you cannot do something to cope with stress in a healthy manner. Simply changing the way you look at a situation can improve your wellbeing in a huge way. For one thing, it allows you to deal with a problematic situation in a more fulfilling manner and avoid suppressing your angry feelings.

Cognitive reappraisal combined with empathy can help you bounce back from any setback. For example, appraising the death of a loved one as a part of life rather than resorting to the hollow 'he/she is in a better place' will make it easier for you to deal with your feelings, which are usually those of helplessness and lacking control. And when you are a parent, the way you deal with stress like losing a loved one impacts your children a lot. Finding a palatable way to reframe a problem so that you can deal with the feelings it brings allows you to maintain your level of wellbeing.

Stop stressing about lack of sleep

Lack of sleep can make even the most cheerful clown become gloomy. When you are bringing up a young child, you can expect to be disrupted by cries at every turn, even when you are most desperate for sleep. Sleeplessness becomes an even worse problem when you start stressing about it. This only exacerbates the problem and makes it more likely for you to experience the adverse effects you fear so much. It is the old problem of stress activating your fight or flight responses.

The stress-sleeplessness circuit is especially grave when you are a child. First off, you are worried right off the bat that your child's midnight cries will deny you the chance to sleep. These negative thoughts make it harder for you to sleep when you get the chance because you are afraid of the moment your child wakes up. Your child senses your worry and responds the only way they know how to – by crying. This completes the self-actualizing loop of parental stress and sleeplessness. Rather than get caught up in this loop, it is more helpful for you to find practical ways of solving problems with sleeplessness. A proactive mindset when you are dealing with any problems means that, at some point, you will discover a workable solution.

Look out for yourself

Most parents make the mistake of dedicating all their energy to their kids and neglecting their own needs. When you stop doing the things you love; the things that make you happy, you make way for the stress of your day-to-day life to get to you. Ultimately, your kids will pay the price because you will become more irritable. The things that give you meaningful pleasure allow you to block the toxic kind of stress from accumulating in your mind.

You should never let your parenting duties come in the way of the things that make you happy. If possible, you can even invite your child to help out, which will become a great bonding moment for you. For example, if you are a lover of nature, you can take time to enjoy the outdoors every week. Even if you cannot spend a whole night camping in the wild, a hike will give you the same sort of wholesome benefits in less time. Pursuing meaningful happiness actively makes your life happier and improves your ability to parent.

Simplify

Sometimes the stress that makes you angry at your child comes from a misguided attempt at taking on so much that there is simply no time to do it all. You should only take on the responsibilities that you can handle and learn to say "no" a lot more often. You should cut out anything that is not essential to your job or your family to make time for the important stuff. Even some parenting responsibilities like PTA bake sales and other non-essential activities can be taking an undue toll on you and giving you fewer rewards compared to fun activities like sporting events or reading with your child.

As much as you might be tempted, resist the temptation to become the supermom. A lot of what the supermom does is made-for-movies anyways. Just being a good mother is enough for your child. It is also doable and will leave you a lot less strained and enjoying your responsibilities as a mother a whole lot more.

Find support

One very effective way of simplifying is to find support for some of your parenting activities. Every spouse should have a quota of responsibilities to take care of, as should your extended family and friends. Any time that you can find to bequeath your child onto another person and take some time to yourself is time that you get to take care of yourself. You should take this time to engage in some meaningful happiness activities.

The parents of your child's peers can also be a great support group, mostly because they understand exactly what you might be going through. Organize a neighborhood carpool and homework clubs to give your child the opportunity to interact with other children his or her age while lessening the time you spend in his or her direct care.

Do not multitask

Like many other parents, you will be tempted to do two or more activities at the same time in the pursuit of efficiency. The only thing that you will succeed in doing is creating a lot of stress for yourself and more mistakes than you will ever have time to undo. You will accomplish a lot more tasks a lot more quickly by focusing on one thing at a time until it is finished.

This goes for attending to your child's needs too. You should be sure to spend at least fifteen minutes of distraction-free time with your child where there are no phones and no television. Children who receive positive attention from their parents exhibit a higher level of cognitive functions and concentration. Focusing on your child's needs will also help you to notice when they are struggling with something so that you can deal with it before it becomes an issue.

Embrace imperfections

A lot of the stress that parents feel comes from the notion that everything you do must be perfect. No matter how good of a job you are doing, your inner critic will always be disapproving. The harder you try to become perfect, the further you will get from finding happiness and satisfaction. Give yourself a break, allow yourself to make mistakes, and embrace your imperfections. If nothing else, the lower level of stress this will bring into your life will allow you to handle your anger a lot better.

The same goes for the way you go about raising your kid. Perfectionist parents make the same sort of impossible demands on their children that they make on themselves. First off, this goes against the basic principles of child psychology, which is that children think and go about life quite differently from adults. Secondly, you will find yourself angry most of the time because nothing your child does will ever be enough. You should teach your child to do the best that they can do in everything that he or she does. As long as she or he keeps improving on this, then they stand to grow into an outstanding adult.

How to Deal With an Angry Child

Parental anger management goes beyond improving your wellbeing as a parent. As important as parental well being is, it does not make up for being clueless as to how you are supposed to handle your angry child. And like I mentioned in chapter 2, parental and child anger are intertwined. If your child is angry, he or she is likely to pass the anger on to you with their actions. And when you are angry, you will probably do something to anger your child like screaming at him or her. In this section, we will cover the practical strategies that you can apply in dealing with your angry child.

Delay

This is the most important lesson in handling your anger. Delay your anger for as long as possible regardless of the mistake that your child made. For example, if you are picking him or her up from mall jail, delay the confrontation until you get in the car, then until you get home, and then after a time-out in their room. By the time you get around to addressing the issue at hand, you will have calmed down enough to have a clear head for problem-solving.

Breathing exercises

Take a few calming breaths before dealing with any child-related stress. This allows you to quiet down your stress and stay grounded. Only then can you manage trying moments with your kids in a graceful and calm manner.

Recreation

Sometimes all you need to keep your child happy is some happy moments. When you engage in recreation such as sports with your child, the physical activity acts like a salve to anger and allows both of you to release the frustrations trapped deep within. The time you spend together in play strengthens your connection to your child and facilitates some healthy communication.

Teaching self-expression

Children express a range of emotions like fear, worry, embarrassment, and sadness, among others with anger. For a toddler who cannot speak, this may be acceptable. As your child grows and learns to talk, you should teach him or her how to express their needs, their fears, and their worries. Question your child about his or her feelings when they are upset so that you can become more adept at interpreting their frustrations. A good sense of self-expression will help your child to talk about issues that bother him or her instead of getting angry.

Healthy communication

Sometimes a child will get angry because he or she needs to feel heard and seen and she is not getting that from the world. It is your job as a parent to listen and observe. If your child is doing something, you should be the greatest fan. When you are a parent, communication with your child goes beyond words. Children communicate with their body language, their actions, and their performance in school. It is your place to decode everything your child is telling you and move to fulfill their needs.

Understanding/relating

In the spur of the moment when you catch your child doing something naughty, your own adult interpretation of right and wrong tends to take over and override your ability to relate. For example, a two-year old child would not have the smarts to know that flour is not something to play with. You should always try to look at a situation from your child's point of view before handing out your punishment.

Listening

Parents with naughty kids tend to have a lot more trouble with this particular strategy. You assume that your child did it even before you know the situation just because she or he has given you so much grief in the past. What this does is that it makes your child feel like you do not believe in him or her or that you are not on his or her side. Taking the time to listen will also help you to delay acting on your anger when you catch your child in a mistake. Who knows, maybe your daughter or son's impossible explanations will crack you up and bring some comic relief to a tense situation.

Drop your anger

Sometimes you waste your anger on things that are not worth stressing over. With the small things, you can let your child go scot-free. Just be sure not to let this system of overlooking a child's mistake become your way of parenting. You should only ignore the smallest slip-ups.

Forgive

Sometimes it helps to react with compassion in place of anger, especially when you have been interacting with your child through anger a lot. For example, when you need to teach an important life lesson that might help your child change his or her behavior, you can get a lot further over an ice cream than screaming at him or her across the room.

Be the parent

The role of a parent entails providing, protecting, and guiding. It is the same even when you have caught your child in a mess-up. You should be more mature and more level headed so that you can solve the problem at hand. Sometimes your child is only acting out because he or she lacks the knowledge to deal with his or her personal issues. You should offer guidance on how to do so or find a mentor if you are unqualified to deal with a particular problem. Finally, you should be a role model to your child in everything that you do. If you do not know how to handle your anger or if your life is not organized, your child will probably mirror that.

Chapter V: Emotionally Intelligent Parenting

Emotional intelligence is one of the most important skills you need so you can live harmoniously with others. It allows you to get a grip on your impulses and keep a clear head when dealing with conflict. It also gives you the skills you need to maintain healthy relationships with the people around you. Keeping a tight grip on impulses is crucial when you are raising a child because the most harmful expressions of anger are those that happen instinctively. These include name-calling and spanking an unruly child in the spur of a moment. In this chapter, we will focus on the aspects of emotional intelligence that entail understanding and managing your emotions to deal with conflict.

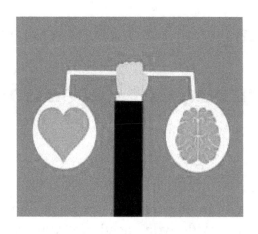

Benefits of Emotional Intelligence

Impulse control

Even with a full understanding of your parenting style, you will be hard-pressed to continue acting in a levelheaded way when you are fuming at your child. A person with a high level of emotional control will understand the need to keep his or her head in charged moments to avoid hurting others. This is what emotional intelligence allows you to become. The higher your level of emotional control, the better the control you will have over your impulses. This means that you will still have the presence of mind to take a moment to gather your wits before you start talking or lashing out when you are angry.

Dealing with crises

Emotional intelligence entails learning how to deal with problems in a sober manner. The ability to do this means that you never have to lose your head when there is a problem because you are confident in your ability to solve it. Feelings of helplessness play a huge part in parental anger, mostly because you are responsible for so much more than your child's needs in the present. After all, the things you do to your child will affect his or her life for years to come. The problem-solving technique of thinking about challenges helps to deal with anger because it gives you something to think about and because it will ultimately give you the solutions that you really need.

The most effective problem-solving technique entails;

1. First, seek to understand the exact nature of the problem. Sometimes our own fears magnify small problems and make them appear bigger than they really are. Define the problem in a statement, then twice more using different words. This allows you to determine what is important in a situation.

2. Come up with a list of solutions to the problem. Brainstorm as many solutions as possible without dismissing any one of them for the time being. Write down these ideas if you are afraid that you might forget them.

3. Go through the different solutions one by one and eliminate those that are non-workable. Narrow down the list of possible solutions until you have the best three.

4. Put the most promising solution to practical use and evaluate how effective it is. If it does not work, tweak a few things and then try out the next solution on your list.

5. Evaluate the whole situation and figure out if you are better off for it. For you to consider a problem solved, the situation should improve significantly and visibly.

Anger and You

As a parent, you will get a lot of advice from friends and family on how you should raise your child. Some of this advice may work, but most of it will probably not be applicable to your situation. Even worse, following some well-meaning advice often makes it even harder for you to execute your parenting duties. This is because you make the mistake of thinking that all parents deal with problems the same way. In truth, parenting styles vary and can be as unique as our different personalities. It is just the same way that children have different personalities and present problems in special ways.

Different parenting styles

Parenting styles fall under four major categories. These four different types of parents handle problems with their children uniquely. However, by default, parents with the same style of parenting will react similarly to problems. This includes the ways that a parent acts when angry and the expectations they have in their children. Understanding your parenting style will help you to improve your ability to manage your anger and to find strategies to help you improve the relationship you have with your son or daughter.

Authoritarian

The authoritarian style of parenting is very strict and firm when it comes to disciplinary matters. Parents lay rules down in a clear and transparent manner and demand total obedience. Any time a child deviates from the right way, an authoritarian parent will not hesitate to enforce justice by bringing the law down on him or her. An authoritarian parent does not respond well to their child challenging them on any score. They tend to react to any form of challenge to their authority with anger.

In handling anger, authoritarian parents tend towards the more forceful techniques of expressing anger. They will rarely ever hesitate before handing out a strict punishment based on a dim view of a child's actions. The authoritarian parenting style is threatening enough on its own, but authoritative parents tend to use threats more than any other tool when they are angry. These threats can be terrifying to kids because they are so scared of the parent already.

If you operate by a very strict set of rules with clearly stated punishments for wrongdoing, then it is likely that you are an authoritarian parent. Another feature of authoritarian parenting is less flexibility in dealing with your child's mistakes. There is no such thing as compassion in the authoritarian parenting kit. The parents make the rules that must be followed at all times and exercise absolute authority. If the voice of the child is not rejected outright, then they are frightened into silence by the way their parents handle dissent.

Children raised by authoritative parents will respond to the constant anger and the strict home life by either withdrawing into themselves or rebelling. Authoritarianism has never been an effective method of wielding power, mostly because people tend to appreciate freedom and resent any form of restriction placed upon them. You should temper your demeanor a little and give your child some say in their own lives, even if you do need to make rules and enforce them.

What the authoritarian parent needs to do is improve the way they communicate with the child. Sometimes, all your child needs is to feel that you are meeting his or her needs. Another thing you should do is invite negotiation when handing out punishments for mistakes. As long as your child does not fear you or feel like you are imposing your absolute rule on him or her, they will be less likely to rebel later on.

Authoritative

The authoritative style of parenting features high demands but is one of the most responsive when it comes to addressing the needs of the child. An authoritative parent will ask a lot out of the child but follow these expectations through with a good measure of love and support. When it comes to disciplining wayward children, authoritative parents are fair and accommodative. This kind of parent will take into account the opinions of the child on issues affecting him or her and thrash out issues on a level bargaining ground.

Authoritative parents handle anger in a child-centric manner, considering what the child has to say about mistakes and rule-breaking before dishing out a fair punishment for wrongdoing. At the same time, authoritative parents explain a child's mistakes to him or her before punishment. The punishment entails making up for the wrong done, and penalizing the child for it. Authoritative parents use punishments like making the child apologize to a wronged party, grounding, and other such teachable actions.

The only thing an authoritative parent needs to watch is that they retain the authoritative style of parenting because it is quite objectively the best style there is. You should watch out for those moments where you slide closer to authoritarianism. You should also be careful not to become too accepting of your child's behavior as to be permissive.

Permissive

Permissive parents demand very little of their children even when they remain highly responsive to their needs and support them any way that they can. A permissive parent will make his or her child feel loved and cherished while at the same time allowing them to do most of whatever they wish to do. In this way, a permissive parent becomes more of a friend than an authority figure. They also enable their children's conduct by letting them get away with most deeds.

Because of the few demands that permissive parents have on their children insofar as acting in a 'mature' way or getting a particular grade in school, they rarely ever get angry at their child's behavior. When a permissive parent gets angry, it is usually because the child has gotten into some serious trouble. However, most of the time the parent will direct his or her anger elsewhere and not at the child. For example, they might justify a child's lack of completed homework assignments by saying that it is the fault of the school for not enforcing homework rules. Or that the police are picking on a minor by cuffing their hands when arresting him or her.

When a permissive parent is confronted by the child's wrongdoings because of their failure to enforce rules, they tend to adjust and become a lot more authoritarian or move into uninvolved parenting. Because there is no established line of authority between the parent and the child, children tend to respond to a permissive parent's anger with indifference or scorn.

To avoid having your son or daughter develop poor judgment, aggression, and delinquency, among other bad behaviors, you should avoid the permissive style of parenting from the onset. It is important that you establish yourself as the authority figure for your child and teach him or her how to live. Usually, this lack of confidence in one's ability to raise a child is what makes a parent permissive. Overcome your confidence issues and establish a support system in which your child can grow and thrive. For a permissive parent, strong emotions (other than love) are usually lacking. Starting with a little discipline and a little more structure is the way to go.

Uninvolved

Even worse than the permissive parent is the uninvolved parent who is neither responsive to a child's needs nor demanding. The children of uninvolved parents either will take care of themselves or be raised by hired help and family. An uninvolved parent will often be too busy with their career or personal life to take the time to follow up on their child's progress. The level of involvement (or lack thereof) varies from parent to parent, but the most an uninvolved parent demands of their kid is usually to be home by a specific time. Sometimes uninvolved parents will use money as a tool to control a child's behavior.

In some cases, parents make rules but leave the children to follow them at their sole discretion. The parent's extent of anger will then be limited to the child's adherence to the unenforced rules, which might happen only occasionally. Children raised by uninvolved parents tend to indulge in irresponsible behavior in a cry for help. Their actions are usually motivated by the fear and anxiety of having little to no parental guidance to fall back on when dealing with stress.

Together with the permissive parent, the problem with the way an uninvolved parent handles anger is that there is not enough of it to begin with. Uninvolved parents need only become involved if they have any sort of emotional investment in their child's life. The reason why an uninvolved parent will rarely ever get angry with their child is that there is little emotional investment there in the first place.

The mixed-style parent

Some parents combine aspects of the four parenting styles over time. This ever-changing parenting style is called mixed style parenting. Depending on how you apply it, the mixed style method of parenting can be a good thing or be very bad.

One way that parents apply the mixed method of parenting is letting their personal lives such as career dictate the way they parent. For example, you can become very uninvolved because you are struggling at work or with your business, or you and your spouse are too engrossed in marital fights to notice your child's struggles. When a parent deviates from one style to another from time to time, they risk damaging the emotional harmony established with their children in the "off-time". Your child will start to feel like he or she is secondary to whatever you neglect his or her needs for, or that they are dispensable.

The only time when the mixed style method of parenting might be necessary is when you are raising a few children with different personalities. You must cater to the needs and demands of each child without making them feel suffocated or neglected. Moreover, you are supposed to adapt your parenting style to the growing needs of your child. If she or he grows up to become more independent than they were in the early years, it is more constructive to adjust accordingly. For example, young adults tend to assert their independence by wanting to engage in activities that are more "grown-up". If you do not give him or her permission to do this, they will go behind your back and probably face more risk that way. The trick in determining the way you parent is to look at the needs of your child and adjust accordingly.

Emotional Intelligence for Your Child

Emotional intelligence is not just a technique that a parent might use to manage their parental anger. It gives anyone who has mastered it the ability to express his or her emotions in a clear and efficient way. It also allows for the mastery of emotional self-control, which means that you can figure out the things that you ought to say in front of people and those that you should hold back. Children normally have none of these skills and unless you teach your child to express himself or herself properly from a young age, they might never master these skills.

Emotional intelligence allows a child to solve problems in a creative manner as well as put up with the emotions of others, especially when these emotions are negative. When you teach your child emotional intelligence, you teach him or her that feelings serve the purpose of making us know what we want. This way, a child learns to appreciate his or her feelings and to respect other people's emotions. The most important aspect of teaching emotional intelligence is training your child on the effective strategies of dealing with negative emotions.

Parents deal with their children's negative emotions through one of the four methods namely; dismissing, disapproving, acceptance, and emotional coaching. Dismissive parents put little stock into the emotions of their child and try to get rid of them as soon as possible. In a dismissive parent's point of view, a child needs only experience joy. Any time they display a different emotion a dismissive parent will use any distraction available to entertain the child back into happiness.

Disapproving parents rarely take the time to appreciate their child's feelings. At the first sign of negative feelings, they do everything possible to quash it by punishing the child. Punishments will often grow harsher as the child's unexpressed emotions grow stronger and their expression more frequent.

Acceptance is pretty much how permissive parents deal with their children's negative emotions. They simply accept anything the child does without questioning or seeking to find the cause or possible solution for it. These parents are also called laissez-faire because they do not teach problem-solving or put any sort of limitation of a child's expressions of negative emotions.

Finally, we have the emotional coaching strategy of dealing with your child's emotions. This strategy views every expression of feelings as a teachable moment and emotional coaching parents will usually take moments of emotional expression to connect with their child. By pointing out how doing something can be bad for the child and other people, you empower him or her to rise above it and learn how to express themselves better.

Emotional coaching

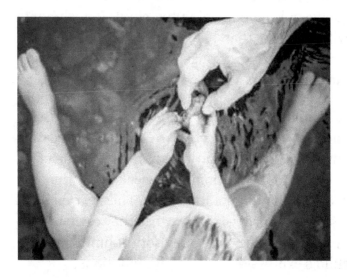

If there is one thing that you must take away from this book, it should be that your child's emotions are important. This includes the emotions that follow your actions after your child has done something wrong. In fact, children make the most significant choices when their emotions are raw. You must be careful to ensure that these choices are the right ones for your son or daughter.

The five steps for emotional coaching

1. Notice your child's emotions. It is very important that you keep observing and reading into your child's actions and words. The best way of coaching your child to manage his or her emotions is to acknowledge them before he or she starts to express them. This gives you the time to figure out how best to handle the moment when your child finally expresses the emotions.

2. Take the opportunity to strengthen the connection you have with your child. Find the best possible way of addressing your child's feelings and go with the most fun and pleasurable way of doing it.

3. Validate your child's feelings. No feeling can ever be wrong because all feelings are simply meant to show us what we need. Try to relate by actually putting yourself in your child's shoes. If you can relate with something from your own life, that might deepen the connection.

4. Clarify what the emotions indicate. As the parent, you are supposed to bring clarity to

your child's confusion. You should label the emotions your child is going through.

5. Guide your child to solve the problem at hand. The problem-solving step of dealing with negative emotions is very important for building character. If you handle everything for your child, you risk making him or her too reliant on your protection to handle his or her own problems. Focus on teaching the skills of problem-solving and giving clues rather than giving solutions.

Chapter VI: Common Mistakes in Managing Parental Anger

In this chapter, we will look at some of the common mistakes that parents make when dealing with their parental anger. And because we have already established the close relationship between parental and child anger, I will touch on mistakes parents make in dealing with a child's anger as well.

1. Dealing with your child's anger like an adult's

As we mentioned before, children get angry quite differently compared to adults. When you get angry, it is usually because you are annoyed at someone or something. While adult anger can be caused by underlying causes like stress and frustrations, it is very different from child anger. An angry child is usually projecting a whole different set of emotions through anger. You should be observant enough to notice it when your child is simply acting on other emotions like fear or shame through anger. The key is to try to identify the need your child is trying to express through anger and deal with that rather than fighting their anger.

2. Too much tough love

Some well-meaning parents treat their child's grievances with a "well, tough luck" kind of attitude. They expect the child to figure their problems out and deal with pain from an early stage so that she or he is well prepared for life afterward. The danger to this strategy is that you risk making the mistake of becoming callous to your child. Because you are used to seeing him or her dealing with smaller problems, you fail to respond when he or she really needs you. Moreover, some apparently small problems that you might be tempted to let them figure out for themselves will be distressing to your child. A child might grow resentful when he or she feels like you do not care about their suffering. This will create a strain in your relationship and affect the emotional connection you share with the child.

3. Letting your child get his/her way all the time

Some parents who use the dropping strategy of dealing with anger only succeed in allowing the child to have their way all the time. Even worse, they leave their children's mistakes unaddressed instead of taking the moment to teach some lessons on emotional expression. When you fail to respond to your child's negative emotions and at the same allow him or her to have their way, you only succeed in reinforcing the child's behaviors. You have to teach that there are consequences to actions regardless of the anger it arouses in your child. As long as you educate your child on ways of dealing with anger, you should reinforce the lesson that actions have consequences as much as possible.

4. Bribing the child

Some parents are afraid of getting their children angry to the extent of bribing them with toys, money, and treats to get them to calm down when they are angry. Not only does this get you nowhere insofar as teaching emotional expression is concerned, but also you reinforce the notion that your child can use anger to get his or her way at any time. This is how people learn to become emotional manipulators. Especially when your child's actions were negative, the only way to set him or her straight is to enforce positive behavior through discussion or grounding. Your compassion should never get beyond understanding and relating to rewarding (or in any way appearing to tolerate) negative behavior.

5. Handling your anger wrongly

Before you can start dealing with your errant child, take a few moments to collect your thoughts. Try to think about what might be making your child act out and see if there is a way of addressing the root cause of your child's naughtiness. The last thing you want to do is punish your child while she or he is expecting to get some gratitude or support. For example, when a child messes up around the house, it could be a badly executed attempt to help. However great the damage, you do not want to seem to dissuade a child from taking the initiative to get things done.

6. Trying to make your child happy

This may sound like a contradiction, but when you apply it to managing your child's anger, it makes perfect sense. The most common mistake parents make is reacting to their child's frown, whining, or crying by trying to make the child happy again, instead of understanding the feelings behind it. When you do this, your actions are only meant to cheer the child up instead of fulfilling the need your angry child is trying to express. Instead of trying to make the child happy, focus on meeting his or her needs. When this happens, they will be cheerful by default – and you will have succeeded in strengthening your connection even more.

7. Hyper-criticalness

Hyper-criticism is one of the most common ways that frustrated parents express anger at a child who has been constantly in the wrong for a long time. This is especially frequent when a parent is internally comparing a child with a well-behaved sibling. The problem with hyper-criticism is that it makes a child feel like there is nothing they can do right. When the situation reaches this point, a child might decide to simply go wild and break all the rules because she or he will get nagged anyways. This is why it is so much harder to stop criticizing a child once you start. They will give you enough material to ensure that you are doing it for a long time – or until you address the underlying issues.

8. Shaming

Some parents resort to shaming errant children when they are angry. The logic behind this strategy is that when you shame a child, you will force him or her to change their behavior for the better to save their pride. Shaming follows any one of a million strategies, including withholding praise and actually calling out your child on perceived wrongdoing. Shaming is one of the leading causes of child anger directed at their parents. It makes a child feel like they have to work to earn your love, which often never comes because you keep raising the bar. Shaming negatively affects a parent-child relationship and can damage future relationships between the child and others. Even worse, shaming creates some of that anger that lasts throughout a child's life.

9. Shunning

This is one of the most callous ways of dealing with parental anger. It entails removing a child that has angered you from family activities like family dinner or movie night. The shunned child is then expected to learn from the experience to become a better person. In reality, you only succeed in making your child feel picked on and rejected. This complete lack of empathy makes a child more likely to rebel or engage in aggressive conduct.

10.   Threats

Child psychologists have established that threats are just as terrifying for children as a beating. Even worse, because some parents perceive threats as being harmless, they tend to be harsher and more callous. Threats constitute a form of emotional terror campaign directed at the child.

At some point, the child learns to lock out the threatening words as well as the parent's voice. You can keep threatening and intimidating the child, but she or he will only be half-listening. As soon as you are done, the child goes right back to doing what you were angry about in the first place. It also means that any attempts you make at helping your child to modify his or her behavior will, quite literally, fall on deaf ears.

11. Spanking

Like any other aggressive form of expressing anger at a child's conduct, spanking only succeeds in making the child resentful and bitter. When the child was using the mischief as a cry for help in the first place, spanking makes them feel misunderstood and uncared for on top of it all. Spanking will make the child shut down their emotions and repress them, or it will make them become aggressive and take their anger out on other children, people, toys, or themselves.

12. Dealing with mistakes immediately

Parents often make the mistake of punishing a child for mischief as soon as it happens. But this field-justice kind of strategy is fraught with dangers. For one thing, your anger is usually at the boiling point at that time. There is a 99% guarantee that your first instinct in punishing your child for his or her sins will be wrong. Always take the time to calm down and think rationally before addressing the issue at hand. A clear head gives you the opportunity to think about the need your child is expressing through his or her actions. Even as you hand out your punishment for his or her mistakes, you can address the problem and reduce the chances of a similar incident happening again.

13. Losing your temper

It does not matter if you have addressed an issue or made a rule before. The sin your child committed does not matter either. You should never lose your temper, especially in front of the child. The things that we do when we are seeing red are always excessive. You will end up dishing out some severe punishment for very small wrongdoings and do it with little to no compassion. Even the smallest things can arouse a red-hot temper, and it takes a while to work it all out of your system.

14. Being inconsistent

Another mistake that parents make is being unpredictable in their anger. Your child should have a clear idea of accepted behaviors and the things that make you angry and never have to guess how you might react to something. Inconsistency breeds confusion, which in turn disorients the child's idea of right and wrong.

15. Lecturing

Lecturing is often seen as a safer alternative to other aggressive ways of angry communication like threats and shaming. However, it entails talking down at your child, which makes him or her feel picked up on and domineered. All your communications with your child –errant or not – should be relational.

Conclusion

There you have it – a complete breakdown of anger as it pertains to parenting and its effects on your relationship with your child. We have learned quite a lot.

We feel angry when we feel threatened, when we feel powerless, or when we are anxious about something. Because for some people, one of these feelings will be present at various points of the day, anger can be very confusing and that is why most people fear it.

As a parent, you will be triggered to anger by many of the things that your child does, including lying, ingratitude, wasting (your) time, and poor performance. Stress from your personal and professional life might also cause you to be a lot more angry at your child. The way you handle these issues will largely determine the kind of relationship that you have with your child.

If you do not handle your parental anger in a healthy manner, it will cause the child to have issues later on in life. These issues include aggressive behaviors, lack of empathy when dealing with others, poor judgment in making life choices, run-ins with the law, and the continued perpetuation of parental anger over generations of descendants.

In chapter four, we discussed some of the correlations between parental and child anger, to wit, the fact that anger in a parent will ultimately lead to anger in the child and vice versa. As a parent, you must first understand that a wide range of underlying emotions in the developmental, behavioral, emotional, and social areas of your child's life is what brings about his or her anger.

Some of these causes include physical and emotional hurt, sadness, fear, developmental frustrations, guilt (even for things for which they are not responsible), embarrassment, and conditions like ADHD. It is your job as the parent to figure out the underlying causes of anger for your child and help him or her to work them out. This requires that you drop your anger at your child and first respond to their needs.

An angry two-year-old child will express his or her anger differently from how a nine-year-old will. Keeping up with your child's emotional needs will allow you to remain focused on their different styles of expressing anger. This is especially important when these styles evolve. But your continued support and understanding of your child's mannerisms will boost your relationship by making you a more relatable parent.

Injecting the principles of emotional intelligence to your parenting can have a huge positive impact on the way you relate with your child. Not only does it help you to deal with the impulse to lash out when you are angry with your child, but it also helps you to adopt a more problem-solving strategy of dealing with issues with your child. This boosts your parenting abilities and allows you to cultivate a healthy relationship with your child.

It is also important to teach children emotional intelligence, especially the self-expression aspects of it. An emotionally intelligent child will be easier to parent because she or he will be more capable of communicating their needs instead of acting them out. When you are teaching your child emotional intelligence, you become his or her coach, showing them the ropes of dealing with complex emotions.

References

Bhave, S. Y., & Saini, S. (2009). *Anger management*. New Delhi: Sage Publications.

Brandt, A. (2016, June 1). 4 Reasons Why You Should Embrace Your Anger. Retrieved January 28, 2020, from https://www.psychologytoday.com/us/blog/min dful-anger/201606/4-reasons-why-you-should-embrace-your-anger

Davis, D. L. (2004). *Your angry child: A guide for parents*. New York: Haworth Press.

Markham, L. (2012). *Peaceful Parent, Happy Kids: How to stop yelling and start connecting*. New York City: Penguin Publishing Group.

Mind Tools Content Team. (2017, October 3). What Is Anger?: Understanding a Strong Emotion. Retrieved January 28, 2020, from https://www.mindtools.com/pages/article/what -is-anger.htm